T0381226

AuthorHouse™
1663 Liberty Drive
Bloomington, IN 47403
www.authorhouse.com
Phone: 1 (800) 839-8640

Published by AuthorHouse 02/19/2016

ISBN: 978-1-5049-7304-5 (sc)
ISBN: 978-1-5049-7303-8 (e)

Print information available on the last page.

Any people depicted in stock imagery provided by Thinkstock are models,
and such images are being used for illustrative purposes only.
Certain stock imagery © Thinkstock.

This book is printed on acid-free paper.

Because of the dynamic nature of the Internet, any web addresses or links contained in this book may
have changed since publication and may no longer be valid. The views expressed in this work are solely
those of the author and do not necessarily reflect the views of the publisher, and the publisher hereby
disclaims any responsibility for them.

authorHOUSE®

Travels to Hawaii and Back Home to Houston, Texas!

by Martha Elaine Patrone

This book is dedicated to Joseph Molendyke and the many individuals that have and had suffered from cancer. A portion of the proceeds from this book will be donated to help support cancer research and the patients that it helps.

My first trip to Hawaii was back in 1973 when I was living in Las Vegas and needed a change of venue. I found myself a board a plane and bound for Hawaii with my mind set on becoming a massage therapist. Once I arrived in Hawaii I checked into the Aloha and began my journey to familiarize to local traditions and cultural.

The local people of the island were amazingly friendly and getting to know them was inspiring and rewarding. Each day that I woke up my adventure begin whether it was visiting waterfalls, exotic birds and animals or venturing through the posh rain forest. I began to fall in love with the people and the breath taking views of what the island had to offer. It was like taking a step back in time.

My short adventure of the first trip to Hawaii was short lived and an eager to return back to the island in the near future.

5

World War II Battleship USS Iowa on display at the dock at San Padro. She was built during the early 1940's this 45,000 ton vessel is 887 foot long severed a city at sea for thousands of sailors over three different decades You may tour this great warship.

Before going on board the Princess. I visited my cousin John and aunt Mary in Los Angeles, California. We enjoyed pictures on the computer.

eturning to Hawaii in 2015 was a different kind of experience and this time it would be with my husband and it would be by a cruise ship. Instead of getting on a plane and having a few hours of flight, landing to firmly plant your feet on the ground, the cruise would be non-stop entertainment.

Checking onto the Grand Princess cruise was an experience in itself and when I found my room and walked in and peering out on my deck looking into the midst of the ocean, it was memorizing and breathe taking. Going to the upper decks and watching us sail out of San Padro, California. As we departed into the amazing sunset and my husband and I found that California became a small tiny bit of land mass in the distance. The ocean widens up and the ship was surrounded by nothing but water and we were on our way.

Stevenson Bridge

It was a surprise how hard the ship's crew works around the clock to handle everything from the luggage, room service, the shops the catered to your every possible imagination was there to make your voyage desirable and memorable.

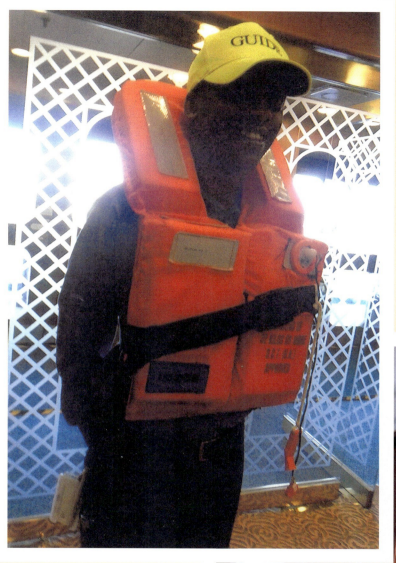

Before sailing there was a drill where they explained the safety feature of the ship.

The evening dinner was filled with so many choices and many combinations. Strolling around the multiple decks to see where everything was located and to see where my husband and I would be spending the next 5 days to reach Hawaii.

They did not have the flow rider on the Princess like they did on the Royal Caribbean.

The next day we awakened to a glorious day and started off by attending the breakfast buffet and once again everything you could possibly imagine to eat. The entertainment that was aboard the ship was a way of occupying and trying new stuff. The lounging around on the decks soaking up the sun and relaxing by treating myself to wonderful massages made my 5 days go by very fast. My husband enjoyed the deck the most. The shows performed on the ship provided indoor cooler entertainment to refresh yourself from the heat of being on the outer decks. Swimming provided a way to enjoy the daytime and the evening while watching the movies on the big screen.

Chef's Day in the theater. I enjoyed this chocolate cooking demonstration. The best part of the show was sampling the chocolate creations.

The art of the Grand Princess!

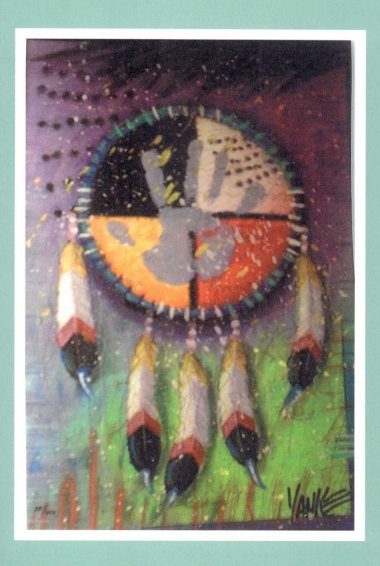

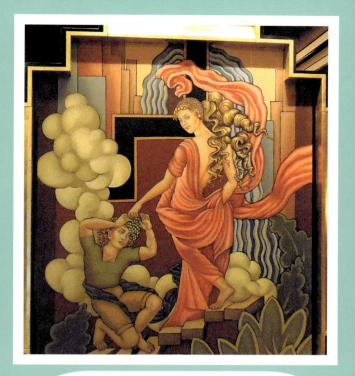

17

Arriving in Hawaii we arrived at the big island, Oahu and ventured off the ship and went site seeing. The botanical gardens were beautiful and lush with greenery. The beautiful banyan trees were in the square. The people were shopping and lounging around enjoying their day. The day was hot and yet, cool breeze flowed on the island as we toured and a sense of how much the island has changed since my first trip 42 years ago. Enjoying the Hawaiian and Tahitian dancers with their grass skirts and the way they embraced the cultural dance was impressive to watch while Waikiki Beach made the closure to the day. I visited the main island viewed the volcanos by helicopter and was very glad to be back on the ground.

Tahitian dancers performing many of the native Hawaii cultural dances.

23

Cooling off from the hot day in Maui, with a ice cool drink!

Banyan trees in Maui are beautiful with the branches growing into the ground.

Everyone is enjoying Maui just look at those smilies!

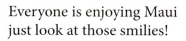

25

The next stop in the Hawaiian Islands
was Maui. Back on the ship we attended
a presentation of the island. Arriving
in Maui and off the ship we go. We
encountered a nice host under the grass
umbrella hut with a friendly face and
conversation about the island. The
morning was a breathe taking. The food
was to be delightful and enjoyable as we
passed our day away. Oahu and Kauai were
our next islands on our journey and more
memorable sights to see. The shops were
lined with hand carved tiki heads designed
with many tribal faces.

Relaxing on the deck is fun while watching whales, dolphins and porpoises. Watch this great ship move across the Pacific ocean is peaceful and relaxing. I did notice the waves get pretty high.

We enjoyed the outstanding violinist performing during one evening entertainment.

Hawaii is not always sunny and beautiful we did have our share of cloudy days.

Sunny days brought out the wonderful vibrant colors of the Hawaiian plants.

Lou Patrone enjoying the many delicious foods found on the ship.

Lou Patrone relaxing in the gardens of the city Maili, Hawaii.

Making new friends is important and fun.

33

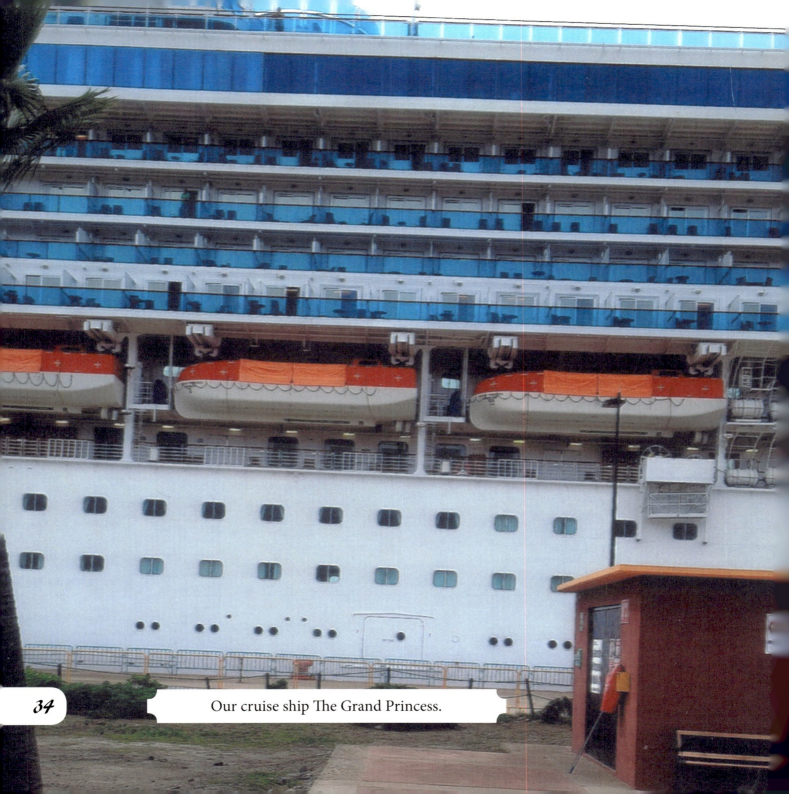

Our cruise ship The Grand Princess.

The Piazza.

This ivory good luck charm worn by native represents the wearer rides the sea and keep them safe.

Waikiki Beach, in Honolulu, Hawaii.

Introduction to Maui in ship theater.

A pretty girl traveling with her mom and dad.

Our nice waitress in Maui, under grass umbrella.

The nightclub is busy and entertaining!

One morning in Hawaii the temperature was a chilly 60° to be exact.

We had Scottsmen posing for photos.
They were wearing kilts, tipical dress
of the men.

Sixty foot tall palm tree providing cooling shade while the nice sea breezes blow gently through the palms.

The artwork on the ship!

The theater had a demonstration of native folk dances. These beautiful ladies performs many of Hawaii's cultural dances.

Maui Hawaii is filled with great places to dine. The Hut is one such place. Great food and service with a beautiful tropical environment.

The Princess ship's smoke stacks are artfully hidden. Smoke rises when this great ship is in transit.

Ohau's Pilot boat guides the Princess to the dock of Ohau, Hawaii.

A local store in Kaui had many different styles of Tiki artwork.

Passenger enjoying the view as the ship docks in Honolulu.

Near the end of this amazing cruise I toss my lei and it formed a shape of a heart. A fitting good bye to a wonderful Hawaii.

Louis and Martha Patrone enjoying the last few days of the wonderful cruise.

Good bye Hawaii I am glad to go home to Houston, Texas. This adventure was full of fun and new experiences.

I will miss this great pool!

Cute baby and father I met at airport while waiting for the plane.

On the way back home we made a stop in Ensenada, Mexico
for a brief time but the time spent in there wasn't as enjoyable
as the time spent in Hawaii. The islands have all changed
and modernized from the first trip there by the buildings and
population. It became a new experience but still enjoyable. Time
now was spent sailing back to Houston, Texas to be back in my
own bed and to see my adorable Shih Tzu's and the puppies that
I had left to go to loving Hawaii.

Teresa and Lou the loves of my life.

Downtown in Fulshear, Texas celebrating St. Patrick's Day. Great fun. I was here for a book signing of my first book called "Spice Princess the Talking Shih Tzu". You can order my first book at www.spiceprincessthetalkingshihtzu.com.

The pups have grow and are already to go to their new homes.

Pups at play with the Prince and Princess over looking.

Back home! Glad to be home with Spice Princess and Prince Charming, her mate.

Martha Elaine Patrone lives in
Houston, Texas. She believes
in living life to the fullest and
helping others in need.

Printed in the United States
By Bookmasters